T0198963

evoking motherhood

a pregnancy journey

CHRISTINE M GALLANT

Balboa Press books may be ordered through booksellers or by contacting:

Balboa Press
A Division of Hay House
1663 Liberty Drive
Bloomington, IN 47403
www.balboapress.com
1 (877) 407-4847

ISBN: 978-1-9822-4988-5 (sc)
ISBN: 978-1-9822-4989-2 (e)

Library of Congress Control Number: 2020911262

Print information available on the last page.

Balboa Press rev. date: 06/22/2020

BALBOA.PRESS
A DIVISION OF HAY HOUSE

Christine Gallant was recommended to us by a close friend when we were expecting our first daughter in 2002. We both come from large families, who were far away and not able to guide us as newly expectant parents. Christine's warmth, knowledge, and quiet strength was a support we did not even realize we needed. Again, in 2004, with an unexpected different birthing experience, our second daughter was born. Christine was with us every step of the way, guiding and supporting us through all that comes with these journeys. When we reflect on those times, Christine is a prominent part of our memories and wonderful experiences for both monumental occasions.

- Cheryl and Lesra Martin

Dreams do come true. My children. Justin, Quinn, Sienna.

I dedicate this book to Doug who has been a constant source of love in my motherhood journey.

WELCOME TO MOTHERHOOD.

You are a home for your baby. Creating a way of being is a gift to your child each day. Set aside time and intention to become stronger in who you are and clearer about what you want for you and your child. Clarity about what is most important to wellbeing becomes your guide.

What is wellbeing?
Nourishment.
Relaxation.
Connection.

Know that you are not alone in wondering how to go about this exactly.…...

Trust that you can find nourishment in physical, emotional and spiritual ways.

What helps you to relax each day?

Who do you feel connected with that you can share this journey?

Each day gives you time to contemplate, practice and evolve into motherhood.

let's get started: a 30 day discovery

Each day you are given:

A contemplation

An activity for you to do today

An activity you can do with your child, one day

A mantra for this day

DAY 1

YOU ARE A MOTHER.

Like a gift being slowly unwrapped by you, nature is giving you paper and ribbon moments as you take on your new role one day at a time. The unfolding of motherhood.

For you, today:
Look through photos of yourself as a baby.

For your child, one day:
Put out toy mother and baby animals. Let your child match them to each other and help name them. Example: The mother is a doe. The baby is a fawn.

Your mantra for this day:
I am a mother.

DAY 2

YOU CREATE A HOME FOR YOUR CHILD.

A robin builds a nest. A fox finds a den. Discovering your own sense of motherhood, you make a place for your baby to sleep and fold tiny clothes ready to be worn one day. Your child is also soaking up today's loveliness as you take in nourishment, sights of beauty, uplifting song and feel kindnesses around you.

For you, today:
Take a walk in your neighborhood where people have homes. Know that you are starting to create the one you want for your child.

For your child, one day:
Build homes out of playdough for toy animals or draw houses and glue people cut outs into doorways and windows.

Your mantra, for this day:
I create a home for my child.

DAY 3

YOU ALLOW YOUR BODY AND MIND TO QUIET.

Monks and nuns enter a place of quietude through meditation or prayer expressing an inner peace that envelopes them in this practice. Finding calm is important just like good nutrition.

Throughout your pregnancy, enjoy such moments to connect with your child at a deeper level which can then guide your thoughts and actions.

For you, today:
Give yourself some time alone without any busyness and find your own place of stillness.

For your child, one day:
Develop a routine of a daily quiet time. Dependent on your child's age, a length of time to self soothe and be with one's own thoughts discovering compassion for self and others.

Your mantra, for this day:
I allow my body and mind to quiet.

3

DAY 4

YOU INTEND TO LOVE THIS DAY.

Go looking for things to love about life. Have fun noticing what is around you as if you have never experienced it and you are going to know the journey of your child.

For you, today:
Try something new like simple words in another language or drawing with your non-dominant hand.

For your child, one day:
Do a science experiment, even something as simple as watching snow melt, and watch your child's eyes widen at what seems like magic and enjoy being an enthusiastic participant in discovery. Curiosity and repetition breed success in learning.

Your mantra, for this day:
I intend to love this day.

DAY 5

YOU SPRING CLEAN.

Just like opening windows and letting in fresh air, how can you let go of and make new spaces in your life for your child? Rooms ready to be filled with creative energy.

For you, today:
Cut and paste a world for your child making a collage of pictures and words that represent what you want for your child.

For your child, one day:
Make a bedroom collage. The pictures can be a reminder of a warm happy space.

Your mantra, for this day:
I spring clean.

DAY 6

YOU MATTER TO THIS CHILD.

See yourself laying on a grassy knoll by a babbling brook, comfortable under a sunshine breeze. Your baby is going to know the essence of being warm and safe without recalling the specifics of growing in the womb. Your presence as its first home.

For you, today:
Have a nap, a few minutes of closing your eyes, visualizing a favorite relaxing spot.

For your child, one day:
Make dream cards, the front with dream colors and inside any words your child might use to describe a dream.

Your mantra, for this day:
I matter to this child.

DAY 7

YOU GENERATE WISDOM.

In the Lion King story, baby Simba is held up high in Rafiki's hands on Pride Rock. The community of lions look up and knows that this cub is going to lead this kingdom, one day, with the wisdom imparted to him by his parents. Think about women, before you, who had children. Realize that you hold that knowledge. The impact of each mother carries forward and, by understanding what has come before, you can make your decisions.

For you, today:
As you go through this day, recall your mother, grandmothers, aunts, neighbourhood women in your mind's eye. Contemplate and connect with generations of wisdom. Write down the kind of mothering and womanhood you learned from them that you want to emulate in your own life.

For your child, one day:
Help your child to take photographs of things like flowers, trees, an anthill, hive or anything you can find and talk about the wisdom behind these creations. Use words like wonder, where, when, how, why to encourage curiosity.

Your mantra, for this day:
I generate wisdom.

DAY 8

YOU HOLD YOUR CHILD.

Just as you now carry your baby in a protective, nourishing cocoon, one day you are going to hold this child in your nurturing arms. Then you will let go, bit by bit by bit. Navigating first steps. Friendship in preschool-kindergarten-grade one. A first love. Each breakthrough creates a new rhythm in your relationship and your love is the steady beat.

For you, today:
Put some music on and dance flooding your body with endorphins. In this moment you and your child are in sync.

For your child, one day:
Make a butterfly. Half an egg carton for the body. Paint each section a different color. Glue onto two colorful cardstock wings.

Your mantra, for this day:
I hold my child.

DAY 9

YOU ARE FOREVER.

When making a stew, you throw in some of this and that and it is not always the same ingredients. Yet, you create a delicious nourishing meal. So, it is with parenting. Stay in open considering mode rather than judgement. The practice of thinking of what you might do in a similar situation is going to lend itself to a calmer clearer perspective. What is forever is your contribution to parenting.

For you, today:
Notice interactions between parents and their children as you walk around your community. Think about the scenarios you observe and how you might deal with them helping your preparation as a parent. So much written information is available about parenting. Starting today to gather knowledge, your curiosity lends itself to more confidence about your choices.

For your child, one day:
Put out red, yellow and blue paints with a palette for mixing them. Create new colors.

Your mantra, for this day:
I am forever.

DAY 10

YOU ARE UNIQUE.

As snowflakes touch down on the earth, not one is the same just like the billions of people who arrive to our world. Finding and expressing your own unique mothering path comes from stopping and paying attention to your true nature. This behavior acts as a model inspiring your child to explore uniqueness. Including being different from you!

For you, today:
Today, with kind intention, trust your gut feeling and make a decision. How to make a clear choice takes practice. For children and parents.

For your child, one day:
Make a picture of your neighborhood street. Show photos and talk about other unique places in the world.

Your mantra, for this day:
I am unique.

DAY 11

YOU WISH FOR YOUR CHILD...

Imagine a teeny fairy sits on your shoulder, magic wand in hand, ready to grant wishes. Wishes can help you identify your hopes for your child. Their fulfillment's first step. With the making of wishes comes surrender. Put your dreams out there and trust the answer.

For you, today:
Write some wishes down for your baby. Put in an envelope, seal it and check in five, ten, twenty years to see if any of those wishes came to fruition.

For your child, one day:
With your child, make a magic wand. Decorate with stars, hearts, sparkles or any kind of adornment. Remember to surrender to the outcome of any wishes!

Your mantra, for this day:
I wish for my child…

DAY 12

YOU REFLECT ON YOUR LOVE FOR THIS CHILD.

Though you cannot see it with your eyes, from land, a colorful world is at play deep in the ocean. Sunlight shimmering on ripples of sea is a reminder of the beauty below these waves. There is a magnificence in loving someone and it sparkles in the heart with even greater influence when you reflect on that person. Let yourself be a conduit of joy for your baby.

For you, today:
Look in a mirror at yourself and see gratitude. A portal to joy.

For your child, one day:
Decorate around a mirror. Ask your child open-ended questions such as what do we see when we look in a mirror?
(Or make a kaleidoscope with older children)

Your mantra, for this day:
I reflect on my love for this child.

DAY 13

YOU GIVE YOUR CHILD FRESH AIR.

Deep refreshing breaths fill your body, stagnancy swept away making room for the new. Physical and emotional tension is replaced with ease. This same serenity of breath helps you to birth your baby and parent your child.

For you, today:
How many slow breaths can you take per minute? A daily activity of intentional breathing. Before you get out of bed. In the middle of the afternoon. Before sleeping at night. Even one minute giving you positive impact. When preparing for a race, you build day by day for the event. Just as you would not run for miles first time out, so it is with using your breath to relax your body and mind.

For your child, one day:
When there is calm energy, teach your child to take some slow breaths. Fill up the heart and blow happiness out to the world. This practice during a relaxed time helps your child to access and use it more easily in times of distress.

Your mantra, for this day:
I give my child fresh air.

DAY 14

YOU SMILE.

Imagine you are the moon in the sky that wears a smile that shines on those around you. Just smile. Close your eyes and remember a positive experience. Feel your baby's smiling essence surrounding you.

For you, today:
Go out to your driveway, sidewalk or sandy beach and do your own positive messaging to bring a little joy to someone in your community's day.

For your child, one day:
Along your local sidewalk, your child, with you or a friend, can use chalk and draw or write out positive images or words. Knowing that others are going to see these messages is uplifting for everyone.

Your mantra, for this day:
I smile.

DAY 15

YOU ALLOW YOUR TEARS TO BE COLLECTED IN A SWEET BOWL OF COMPASSION.

Raindrops spatter against your window clinging to something solid, trickling down with earth's invite to nourish its ground. When tears flow, be there for yourself. Give kindness that you would offer to another person. Here, right now, in this moment. Being backwards or forwards in your mind uses energy you can be giving to this present moment as you gain comfort in the expression of your own feelings.

For you, today:
Journal your thoughts, expressing how you feel, and then write back to yourself as you would a friend.

For your child, one day:
You are going to see your child feel and show intense emotions. Give a way of expressing what is happening through play. Have a listening ear to what is being said, as your child roleplays, giving insight. In the moment, when your child is struggling with frustrations, limits and consequences, clear confident compassionate interaction is the payoff when you release control and are present.

Your mantra, for this day:
I allow my tears to be collected in a sweet bowl of compassion.

DAY 16

YOU ARE FLEXIBLE.

Trees bend in gusts and gales and your body's muscles lengthen and stretch to bend. So, the limber mind and heart show grace. There are aspects of pregnancy and birthing in which there is no control. Thinking in a flexible way can give support to generate your dream experience. Be ready to reach for the magic while keeping your feet planted firmly on the earth. Create a pregnancy and birth plan to communicate what is important to you and use it as a blueprint.

For you, today:
Write down in a free-flowing way your ideal of your pregnancy and birthing experience. From this expression, make a list to share with your caregivers. Putting yourself in their shoes helps you to expand your own thinking.

For your child, one day:
Set out children's yoga cards and stretch along together. Use the concept of 'Destination Imagination' which is a program where students come together to creatively problem-solve challenges. Gather ideas from this program or come up with one for your own family.

Your mantra, for this day:
I am flexible.

DAY 17

YOU COUNT YOUR BLESSINGS.

Count blessings like stars sliding down a crescent moon falling gently into your hand. Each day, for the rest of your life, you are this child's mother. That is never lost nor is your collection of blessings.

For you, today:
Write what makes you grateful during this pregnancy time. You can add photographs of your pregnant self, beautiful places you visit and inspiring sayings you come across while pregnant.

For your child, one day:
Plant something with your child. Talk about the sun and the moon and how they help things to grow. This is an opportunity to talk about making the world a more beautiful place.

Your mantra, for this day:
I count my blessings.

DAY 18

YOU ARE BEAUTIFUL.

Like rays of sunshine, each beam a different color, your ease fills the room. Know that you are beautiful to this child. Beauty, on an emotional level, is ease. Find refuge in sensing and accepting what you are feeling each day. Let the world fall away as you find comfort in your authenticity.

For you, today:
Simplicity. Spontaneity. Serendipity.

For your child, one day:
Have a do-nothing day. Tell your child there is nothing you need to do.

Your mantra, for this day:
I am beautiful.

DAY 19

YOU SEW YOUR WORDS.

Sew your words like a quilt in which you wrap your baby. Thoughtfulness challenges your consciousness as you increase your awareness of the impact, on others, of your words. This guides your interactions as a person and mother. Children are listening to whatever is going on around them. They are known as sponges for learning. They recognize your voice immediately after being born.

For you, today:
Record yourself reading a story, singing a song, sharing some family history. In the first months, record the sounds of your infant as she babbles, says some first words. Children love to hear or see photos or video of themselves when they are a baby.

For your child, one day:
Handwork, like sewing, is sought out by children. Ideas are beads and string, containers with lids, buttons and zippers. Sweeping, mopping, pouring, open and shutting.

Your mantra, for this day:
I sew my words.

DAY 20

YOU ARE A SCULPTOR.

I am a sculptor forming and fashioning a life experience. As I gently knead my thoughts, carve out time, pattern traditions, a shape forms that is my heart. You are going to use your hands to sculpt so many memories. Homes, meals, gardens. Baths and bedtimes. Picnics and parties and proms. A childhood.

For you, today:
Make pizza, biscuit, cookie, pie or play dough. Notice how you lose yourself in the motion. Your mind quiets. A sense of satisfaction for something you made this day.

For your child, one day:
Sensory experiences have a calming effect. Manipulating material captures attention and becomes meditative. Playdough, plasticine, clay. The sensorial movement helps in the transitioning to mealtimes, bedtimes, events outside the home.

Your mantra, for this day:
I am a sculptor.

21

22

DAY 21

YOU BUILD LANGUAGE FOR YOUR CHILD.

With each word you speak, another piece is added to form a brilliant puzzle of language for your child. As you go about your day chat about what you notice around you. In your belly now and later in your arms, this habit of talking with your child is how you build language. Maria Montessori called this 'the absorbent mind'.

For you, today:
Read to your child, who can hear you! It can be poetry, news, lyrics, children's literature…
(Make some inspiring words on the fridge for yourself with kid letters.)

For your child, one day:
Build a story, taking turns, with your child. Ask open ended questions that spark imaginative responses. Ask your child's opinion.

Your mantra, for this day:
I build language for my child.

DAY 22

YOU TICKLE YOUR BABY WITH LAUGHTER.

Imagine light twinkling around your baby with the sounds of your laughter. Laughing brings an overall sense of well-being.

For you, today:
Watch a funny show, spend time with light-hearted people and look for the humor in everyday situations.

For your child, one day:
Children appreciate the humor of knock-knock jokes. You might want to start your repertoire now.

Your mantra, for this day:
I tickle my baby with laughter.

DAY 23

YOU PAINT THIS DAY WITH VIBRANT COLORS.

Paint your day, mixing up playful colors on your palette and brushing in joy wherever you go! In your mind's eye, wrap your baby in different hues. As you take in the different colors in your surroundings, imagine those spectrums entering your body and filling it with light.

For you, today:
Choose something colorful to wear even if it is only a scarf or piece of jewelry. Fill in your day calendar so that it is a rainbow of experiences that nurture you. Give each one a different hue.

For your child, one day:
Children love to paint, hands squishing or stroking with a brush to splash on colors. A gift of process, not product.

Your mantra, for this day:
I paint this day with vibrant colors.

DAY 24

YOUR HEART IS YOUR GUIDE.

Your heart speaks, pulsing with life force. Your baby hears your heartbeat in the womb. Comforting in its constant cadence. Hold your infant in your heart as you dance the rhythm of this day. Laying against you, when born, your baby is going to hear your heart and know it is you.

For you, today:
Do a sensory integration technique where you take your right hand and touch your left knee and then your left hand to your right knee. As you do this you are marching in place. Notice a sense of balance and calm after a few rounds. Any crossing of midline movement integrates your senses bringing you into mental stillness.

For your child, one day:
From infancy onward, sing nursery rhymes and story songs. Let your child feel and hear rhythm by banging on a drum or pot, clap hands or tapping feet.

Your mantra, for this day:
My heart is my guide.

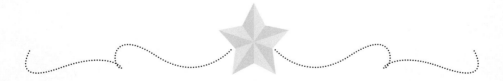

DAY 25

YOU BREATHE IN A MIST OF PEACE.

As your breath flows in and out, in and out, a fine spray of calm falls over you that leaves a mist of peace. Nurture is a gift you give, not only to yourself, but to your child. As you emanate a comfortable presence, your child can feel a sense of home and safety.

For you, today:
Throw yourself a relaxation party! Quench your thirst for calm.

For your child, one day:
Throw your child a relaxation party! Dim lights. Soothing music. Pour a bubbly bath. Comfy clothing. Air warm with cinnamon. A cup of something sweet. A book to bring soft smiles. Quench their thirst for calm.

Your mantra, for this day:
I breathe in a mist of peace.

DAY 26

YOU SPEND YOUR DAY MAKING YOUR ACTIONS YOUR GIFTS.

You are like a turning globe filled with photos of people you encounter each day. You can be a part of creating the kind of world you want for your baby. A compliment given, a thankful note sent, a surprise left on a doorstep.

For you, today:
Find ways, throughout your day, to create kind moments.

For your child, one day:
Help your child to do an unexpected kindness for someone, like shoveling snow for a neighbor.

Your mantra, for this day:
I spend my day making my actions my gifts.

DAY 27

YOU CREATE A POSTURE OF BEING.

Just as you engage your core in physical movement adjusting your posture, so it is with your presence. Step into each morning knowing that with an open heart and steady emotions, you create a posture of being.

For you, today:
Take off your shoes and make footprints. In the sand, snow, water, paint.

For your child, one day:
Create a circle with spokes into a middle spot by making footprints in the snow or sand. Play snow or sand tag. You are safe in the center.

Your mantra, for this day:
I create a posture of being.

DAY 28

YOU WRITE YOUR MOMENTS.

The unexpected is a part of life. Unanticipated, unpredictable, and unforeseen. Just as you rework a storyline, give structure to this day for an uplifting story.

For you, today:
Recall a memory of an experience that you thought would go one way but instead went another and the positive outcome of the situation.

For your child, one day:
Record conversations and playtimes. What a gift to your child, one day, to hear the young self. An audio version of what your child might be saying if old enough to write in a journal.

Your mantra, for this day:
I write my moments.

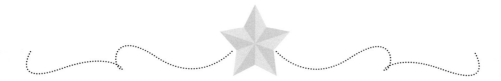

DAY 29

YOU CRADLE YOUR CHILD IN LOVE.

In your womb, your child curls up, held, in safety and warmth. One day, in arms that soothe, with a sway, to and fro, to and fro. In time, hands clasped swinging back and forth, back and forth that brings an ease of spirit.

For you, today:
Go to a space where you can rest, world falling away for a time. A hammock, a swing, or rocking chair.

For your child, one day:
Make a bed out of a shoebox or other container filling it with soft blankets or ferns or leaves. Place something beloved into this cozy space.

Your mantra, for this day:
I cradle my child in love.

DAY 30

YOU JOURNEY IN A SPIRIT OF EXPLORATION.

In the odyssey of a lifetime, just as mother earth revolves around the sun, so you, day by day, move in your exploration of motherhood.

Wanderings and wonderings just as grand as any human adventure. With each unknown, you navigate this world. Not an easy feat, at times but, also, spectacular moments. Body, mind, spirit tested as you discover your soul. The gift of your child's presence.

For you, today:
Take a photo of the sky for your child to see one day, you both, now, under the same stars, sun, clouds, and moon.

For your child, one day:
Go outside and look to the sky. Hold hands and say hello to the morning or goodnight to the moon.

Your mantra, for this day:
I journey in a spirit of exploration.

Printed in the United States
By Bookmasters